100115 1175

These materials may be copied in whole or in part for use in educational
authorities/institutions within the UK, provided that their source is
acknowledged. Under no circumstances may copies be sold, however,
without prior written permission from NCET or the copyright holder
concerned.

Published by NCET in 1993

National Council for Educational Technology
Milburn Hill Road
Science Park
Coventry CV4 7JJ

ISBN 1 85379 213 6

Contents

Acknowledgements

Many people were involved in creating this handbook, and NCET is grateful to them – particularly those who have allowed us to include examples of their work.

Main thanks must obviously go to Chris Dickinson. He was a member of the senior staff of Priory School, Weston-super-Mare at the time the school became involved in pilot work on NCET's Supported Self Study Project. After a period in charge of staff development for Avon LEA's TVEI Project he became Regional Co-ordinator for the Employment Department's Flexible Learning Project in the South West. He is now a Director of Network Educational Press Ltd and a partner in Network Consultancy.

At the time of writing, Julie Wright was National Development Coordinator for Supported Self-Study at NCET.

Other contributions were made by:

Jenny Brown	NCET
John Brown	NCET
David Darwood	Dudley LEA
Peter Gilhooley	Hampshire LEA and The Crookthorn School, Hants
Keith Hemsley	NCET
John Johnston	Strathclyde SRC
Philip Jones	Nottingham LEA
Avril Leigh	Coventry LEA
Christine Patrick	Hyde Sixth Form College, Hyde, Greater Manchester
Ian Smith	The Scottish Council for Educational Technology
Ralph Tabberer	West Sussex LEA
Dianne Tibbitts	Cheshire LEA

The book was edited by Carolyn Gifford, and page make-up was by Jane Osmond.

Julie Wright
NCET

Introduction

Recently the Inspectorate of Nottinghamshire LEA produced a review document entitled 'Differentiation: "not a very familiar word in schools"'. In the short intervening period 'differentiation' has become a much more familiar word as school after school requests INSET on the topic and LEAs produce guidance documents for their teachers.

Undoubtedly the structure of the National Curriculum, based as it is on Attainment Targets and Statements of Attainment, is the driving force behind this interest in differentiation. (For a full examination of the relationship between the National Curriculum and teaching approaches, see *Supported Self-Study at National Curriculum Key Stage 3*, NCET, 1991.)

Whilst some schools are looking to organisational responses to the National Curriculum through the way they group their students, many others are recognising that a more sophisticated response is needed. These latter schools have anticipated that once publicly reported SATs are in place, they will become so rich in information on each student that setting or banding will not on its own deal with the wide variation in ability and attainment in each group. They are therefore looking to a response of changed teaching and learning styles, and this more sophisticated response is at the heart of differentiation.

The purpose of this handbook is to show that achieving a teaching and learning style which allows for differentiation need not be an insurmountable difficulty. Indeed it is hoped that after working through the book, the only thing you will find difficult about differentiation is that it has six syllables! To help you with this, the topic has been broken down into a number of areas so that a starting point should be easier to identify. These areas are referred to as forms of differentiation: within each form a number of strategies are identified using examples that are being carried out by teachers now. The intention is that this handbook will help you to identify some strategies that you can also put into practice now.

What is Differentiation?

Differentiation is a planned process of intervention in the classroom to maximise potential based on individual needs

A planned process

Differentiation doesn't just happen, it is a *planned* process. 'Differentiation implies that the teacher is doing something intentionally . . . thus differentiation is about the planning that teachers do for the characteristics of individuals . . .' (Nottinghamshire LEA)

So differentiation has to be *planned* by you.

An ongoing process

Differentiation is not just an event. 'The commonest characteristics of differentiation between individual learners tend to be an emphasis on dialogue in the form of regular review between teachers and individual pupils about their progress and their learning needs . . .' (Saunders and Weston, *Differentiation in Action: a whole school approach for raising attainment*, NFER, 1991)

So differentiation is *ongoing*. Gloucestershire LEA states that 'differentiation is a process which accommodates differences in the abilities and characteristics of the learner . . . ' (Differentiated support materials for training in secondary schools, 1990). All students show differences. You know from your classes that there is wide variation in:

- the amount of work students complete in a lesson
- the amount of homework they do
- their ability to work cooperatively
- their ability to work independently
- their listening skills
- their presentation skills.

Intervening to make a difference

Allowing these differences to show themselves is not what differentiation is about. Differentiation is about intervening to make a *difference*. As the Warnock report states, 'The purpose of education for all children is the same; the goals are the same. But the help that individual children need in progressing towards them will be different.'

'Whether a class is setted or mixed ability, it will have a range of attainment and interest. The presence of bilingual pupils and pupils with special educational needs further widens the range . . .' (NCC, *Non-Statutory Guidance for Modern Foreign Languages,* February 1992)

In mathematics at Key Stage 3, students will be working on five Attainment Targets between levels 3–8 for each AT. For this subject alone their attainment can be mapped on a matrix with 30 cells in it. The corresponding figures for Science and English are 20 and 30 respectively. Such wide variation in attainment cannot be dealt with organisationally through forms of grouping, and setting or banding will still leave a range of attainment within each class, to say nothing of variations in interest, motivation, aptitude and learning style. Differentiation therefore, is something that needs to happen in your classroom.

Maximising potential

Maximising potential is central to the notion of differentiation, and is the aim of the intervention. It is not the differences between students – these will show themselves anyway. It is the difference between where a student is now and where he or she has the potential to be.

The National Curriculum will help teachers to:

a) assess what each pupil knows, understands and can do
b) use their assessments and programmes of study to identify the learning needs of individual pupils
c) plan programmes of work which take account of their pupils' achievements and allow them to work at different levels
d) ensure that all pupils achieve their maximum potential.

NCC, Information Pack N° 2

We also have to recognise that students have different preferred ways of getting from where they are now to where they could potentially be.

> Differentiation is based on an understanding of individual difference, also the worth and value of each pupil's learning. Because of these fundamental precepts teachers need to differentiate in their curriculum planning.
> Barthorpe and Viner, *Differentiation, your responsibility,* NARE, 1991

Forms of Differentiation

Differentiation is not a single event, it is a *process*. This process involves recognising the variety of individual needs within a class, planning to meet those needs, providing appropriate delivery and evaluating the effectiveness of the activities in order to maximise the achievements of individual students.

The purpose of this handbook is to give practical advice on strategies for providing differentiated learning opportunities in the classroom.

The model below can be used to identify the forms differentiation can take.

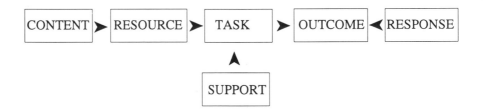

While pupils' outcomes will vary, it is the teacher's *response* to these outcomes that allows differentiation to take place. The content of the curriculum is nowadays defined by statute. To deliver the content of the curriculum, *resources* are necessary and *tasks* have to be designed to enable students to acquire knowledge and understanding as well as developing competences. Whilst working at the tasks, students will have your *support* as you help and guide them through the process.

When your students produce work you will provide feedback to them by correcting and marking that work and by commenting on how it can be improved. In giving different comments and advice to different students according to their strengths and weaknesses, you provide each student with a different *response*.

The remainder of this handbook, therefore, concentrates on those aspects of differentiation over which the classroom teacher has control. These are:

>   differentiation by resource
>   differentiation by task
>   differentiation by support
>   differentiation by response.

Appendices

The appendix contains an interactive exercise on differentiation, checklists, action planning aids and a bibliography.

Differentiation by Resource

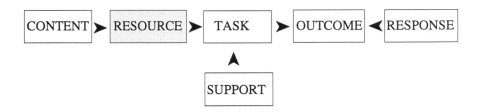

You will already have resources which enable your students to learn the content of your subject area. They may already take the form of individualised programmes such as KMP or SMILE in maths. Alternatively, you may rely on a class textbook. You may also supplement commercially available resources with ones you produce in school.

This section looks at some strategies you might use to enable differentiation to take place through the resources that you make available to your students. These strategies are:

1 Selecting resources for:

- appropriate readability levels
- ease of use
- good design

2 Replacing class texts with a wide variety of media and other sources

3 Use of technology

- tape recordings of key passages
- Concept Keyboards
- CD-ROM

4 Use of study guides

5 Well managed storage and retrieval systems

6 Student preparation

7 Building study skills into course programmes.

Selecting resources

There are a variety of criteria to consider when selecting resources. The two examples below illustrate some of them.

Short sentences

Using the Bible   **Key Stage 3**

1   Open the Bible at any page

2   a)   Find the name at the top of the page. This is the name of the book. (The Bible is made up of 66 different books)
    b)   Find the large black numbers on the page – these are the chapters.
    c)   Find the very small numbers.

3   Now find the reference you have to look up:

   ☞   step 1:   Find the right book   (e.g. Mark)

   ☞   step 2:   Find the right chapter   (e.g. chapter 6)

   ☞   step 3:   Find the verse   (e.g. verse 1)

   ☞   Jesus left that place and went back to his home town, followed by his disciples.

                                              (Mark Chapter 6 Verse 1)

Use of the personal pronoun to appeal directly to the reader

Provision of examples

Clear, explained sequencing of the task

The Life and Times of Jesus

The farmer worked with simple tools.
All the family helped with the jobs on the land .
The shepherd had small flocks of sheep, and they often lived on the hills with the animals.

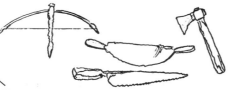

The tekton or carpenter was an important man in the village.
He used tools which were similar to the ones carpenters use now.

Printing is ragged right, but justified to the left to provide visual cues to the next line of text

Selection of language appropriate for the age group

Visual images to improve appeal

Appropriate illustrations to break up passages of text

Pat Davies and the humanities department of Perin's School, Hampshire LEA

Replacing class texts with wide variety of media and other sources

Students differ in the way they make use of these resources to acquire new information. We need to provide a wide variety of media and resources to cater for these differences.

The paragraph below is taken from a West Sussex school. The activity requires students to prepare a school prospectus and consider how it would differ from that for an Indian village school.

Maps

People

The resources needed would be: the school prospectus, large scale plans of the school (from the local studies packs), West Sussex gazetteer for routes to school, atlases/globes/world wallmaps, Action Aid photograph pack on Chebolaki village, database to store and retrieve information about the school, Concept keyboard to annotate school plan and photographs of school here and in India, and English caretaker, cook, ancillary. etc.

Visual Resources

Information Technology

Use of Technology

This example comes from the Flexible Learning in Modern Languages Project in Devon. It makes use of the Concept Keyboard with Touch Explorer software.

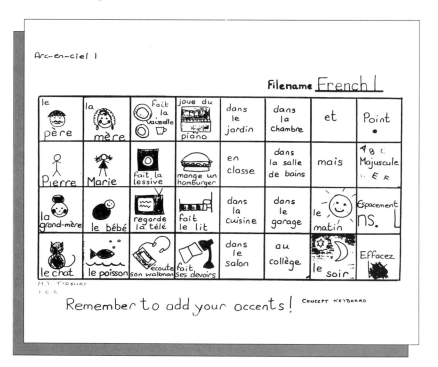

The overlay for the Concept Keyboard enables students to construct sentences in the target language which can subsequently be printed out for them. This enables the student to write in the language irrespective of his or her own writing ability.

This example is taken from the Network Education Press Business Studies Pack.

Margin notes

Activities

Introduction

The changes to the European Community in 1992 is a vast subject. The activities below provide a range of possible investigations. The structure below may help in the planning.

ACTIVITY STRUCTURE FOR '1992'		Optional/ Recommended
Activity 1	Brainstorming/ Listing what is already known	Recommended
Activity 2	Research EC 1992	Recommended
Activity 3	Analysing Research	Recommended
Activity 4	Survey of Community Knowledge	Optional
Activity 5	Survey of Local Business Plans for 1992	Optional
Activity 6	Debate/Discussion involving Community	Optional
Activity 7	Exchange of Information via Twinning Town	Optional
Activity 8	Video Presentation	Optional

Activity 1

Space for student and teacher comments

This activity can be done individually or as part of a small group. Make a list (*or hold a brainstorming session if part of a group*) of what you already know about 1992.
Do not worry about the phrasing or wording of your list – just put the ideas down on paper.
Once you have done this, try to sort your ideas under headings. (*Employment, Trade, Cultural etc.*)

Ideas and stimulus offered

Activity 2

Provides advice on resources

Collect as much information as you can on each of the headings you decide on in *Activity 1.*
Use the sources listed in the Resources section.
If you write to organisations or people, explain what you are doing and what it is you want to know.

Advice provided

'Please send me information on EC 1992' is not enough. **Highlight. Be specific.**
E.g.
'I am interested in finding out more about the laws on employment across the European Community'
When you write, be sure to enclose a large stamped, self-addressed envelope.

Use of Study Guides

Writing resources from scratch takes a lot of time. We know it takes about 10 hours of teacher preparation to produce one hour of student work if we produce the whole learning package. We do not have this time available, so you might look more carefully at the preparation of study guides to go with existing resources.

Well-managed storage and retrieval systems

Where classrooms have a rich variety of resources it is important that the students are able to access the resources when they need them. If the students are dependent on you for the storage and retrieval of resources your time will be diverted away from the important activities of providing differentiation by support and response.

Careful labelling and printing on different coloured paper will help students to manage the use of resources successfully.

Avon Resources for Learning Development Unit developed the use of resource islands to ensure ease of use for students, as shown below.

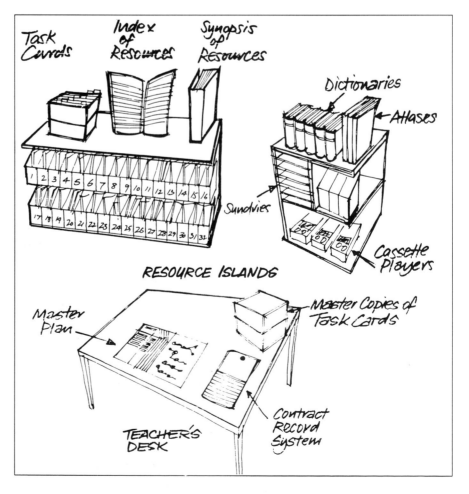

Student preparation

Just as you need preparation for new ways of working in the form of staff development, so do your students. It cannot be assumed that they will cope successfully with new methodologies.

This example, taken from a school in Avon, illustrates how the staff provide induction to Year 7 students embarking on the course. The guide introduces the concept of investment time, i.e. time inserted at the beginning of a new way of working in introducing the methodology rather than covering the content. Like any investment it pays a dividend. The dividend here is in the way students will subsequently be able to meet the expectation set by you. It means that the time you would spend on organisation and control issues is freed for more useful purposes.

Name _____

MY GUIDE TO HUMANITIES

What we shall be exploring

In Humanities our job is to discover as much as we can about humans. We try to answer questions such as:

– What is it about humans which make us human?
– How did we become humans?
– How have humans affected their world?
– How can we become more human and make the world a better home for humans?

How we shall explore

During the year ahead we shall make a number of different explorations on different topics. Some explorations will last one week, others four weeks or even longer. We shall use methods of exploring from the subjects of geography, history, religious and social studies. These will include: visits outside school both near and far; radio and TV programmes; cassette tapes and filmstrips; study kits, books, photographs, diagrams and statistics; surveys, simulation games and drama.

For each exploration you will have a contract or agreement about how much work you will do during the exploration. Everyone will have to complete their contract and there will be a chance to do bonus work in each exploration.

What we shall need for our explorations

As part of your contract you will agree to bring the following six types of equipment to every Humanities lesson:

Humanities Journal   2 lead pencils
Humanities folder   4 coloured pencils or felts
2 ink or ballpoint pens   1 ruler with centimetres

If any equipment is forgotten (you can borrow from friends *before* lessons start) you will be given extra work to be written at home in your own time.

How we shall use our humanities journals

We shall always remember six things:
1   Put headings for each new piece of work.
2   Underline all headings.
3   Put titles on all drawings.
4   Cross out neatly with a ruler like this – ~~wrongly~~
5   Write neatly and waste no space.
6   Do corrections on our Favourite Mistakes Sheet in our folders as soon as our Journal has been marked.

How we shall use our humanities folders

Our folders are for storing our collections (corrections, opposites, places), contracts, answer sheets and projects. Every time you put a new sheet in your folder you must:
–   give it a page number on both sides
–   put the title against that page number in the index at the front of your folder.

How we shall behave

Successful explorers always have two qualities which they need because they have to work together with other people to make their discoveries. These qualities are:

Self-Control   and   *Self-Reliance*

Paying attention   Making your own mind up
                                            as much as possible
Not calling out
                                            Not getting answers from
Discussing quietly   other people.

Doing a fair share of work

Now start your Glossary in the back of your journal by writing and underlining these two phrases and then putting their meanings.

Building study skills into course programmes

In some schools study skills are taught separately from the subject being studied. They might, for instance, be covered as part of a pastoral programme. For some students this raises difficulties in transferring the skills to their subject area.

In this example, again taken from a Network Educational Press study guide, the necessary skills are identified at the point at which they become relevant.

Presentation: General Hints

You need to make your **Final Report** as interesting and informative as you can.

- Aim to maintain interest by variety – this applies whether your presentation is spoken or written.

- Use visual aids – a pie chart, bar-graph, photographs and diagrams, all make a report more attractive.

- Label all diagrams, maps, photographs carefully and say where they came from.

- Remember to include any suggestions for further work that you might have done given the time.

- Describe ways in which you might have improved your study and note any problems you faced when completing the coursework.

When you have finished your work, number all pages and make out a **Contents Page** to put in at the beginning of your report, immediately after your Title Page.

Finally, put in a written 'thank you' (acknowledgement) to all the people and organisations who helped you to carry out your investigation.

Go back and check your work – **Be neat, Be careful, Be organised!**

Differentiation by Task

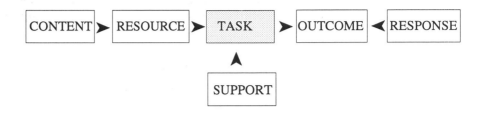

Students work in a variety of ways and bring different abilities and aptitudes to that work. One form of differentiation is to provide a variety of tasks that cover the main content area in order to cater for the variety of individuals in the class.

There are six strategies you might think about to help you with this:

1 Providing an appropriate variety of tasks

2 Matching tasks to student abilities, aptitudes and interests

3 Finding mechanisms to ensure that students stay on task

4 Identification of the outputs tasks lead to

5 Providing a range of tasks to allow choice

6 Building learning routes.

Appropriate Variety

When designing tasks, it is important to allow for different starting points for pupils' varying abilities. Remember also to provide variety in type, level, media, skills and styles.

The example below, from West Sussex LEA, provides several starting points.

Lessons In Mathematics

A   Consider a 'snake' made of matchstick squares.

4 segments need 13 matchsticks

B   Investigate how many matchsticks will be needed for 25 segments and see if you can find a relationship between the number of segments and the number of matches.

C   Pupils can be introduced to the task with a view to reaching the following stages:

start with simple cases (1 segment, 2 segments ...)
look for patterns (going up in threes)
produce a table of results (perhaps a graph too)
establish a relationship/rule
try other geometric snakes (triangles, pentagons, hexagons etc.)
establish a generalisation relating the matchsticks to the number of sides of the polygon
use symbols to represent the generalisation and try extensions like: find the number of segments given the number of matchsticks; even work in 3-D.

Sequencing from simple to complex

Differing levels of task to cope with ability spread

D   An alternative entry point to the activity for the more able would be to reverse the relationship and ask them how many matchsticks given a certain number of segments, perhaps using algebra. Then by moving them on to examining two-deep snakes,

they could start to explore matchstick squares and rectangles, i.e. size related to matchsticks.

Then they could move on to examine more complex growth patterns,

Opportunities for extension

or even 3D ones ...

Matching tasks to students

In the two examples that follow, the first (from Hampshire LEA) shows how an introductory activity in history can be tailored to differing levels of ability; the second (from West Sussex LEA) relates to the example of page 7 and illustrates different methods of grouping.

Consider the nature of the task, and whether it is:

- core or extension
- closed or open
- for individuals, pairs or groups.

Ways of teaching Causation

Different starting points

Case Study: The Peasants' Revolt: Key Stage 3

True/False statements about Causation.

Contribution to the task not dependent on writing skills

Pupils make three piles of these cards
True:
False:
Unsure:

You might wish to **differentiate** this activity by offering pupils some of the more basic cards first, then introduce the more complex ones gradually. Try to encourage pupils to talk about the cards and to resist the temptation to assign them to the piles willy-nilly.

Vary between paired or group work

Events always have more than one cause	The more important events have more causes
If it happened a long time before the event it cannot be a cause	The most important causes happen just before the event
Some causes might be accidental and not planned	Every history book agrees about the causes of an event
The order in which events happen is very important	All events in history are bound to happen (inevitable)
There are some causes which were not very important	People at the time always knew what the causes of the event were
Most events in the past could have been avoided	Things always turn out as people in the past planned
All events that follow each other must be connected	Some causes are more important than others
The connection between causes is important	It is always possible to know all the causes if the historians do their research properly.

Statements allow discussion to proceed at different levels of complexity

15

Allows teacher
to group
students in
different ways
to suit the
purpose of the
activity

The methods used are:

whole class discussion and a synthesis of the issues raised by the whole class, to apply initial criteria to the existing prospectus

paired work on mapping the school using the existing school plan

paired work (pairs chosen by the teacher and by pupils) to interview people in the school

grouped work (3 or 4 maximum) to investigate aspects of the school that arise from class discussion (e.g. jobs, use of rooms, equipment, transport to school etc.)

Whole-class discussion to provide understanding for all members of the class

Opportunity for extension work

Ensuring students stay on task

With the teacher more actively involved in supporting students through small-group tutoring (see the section on Differentiation by Support), it is important to use strategies which ensure that the rest of the group stay on task. One mechanism might involve a learning contract, such as the example below, from Avon LEA.

Name: ....

Humanities Contract 3

Exploring Basic Needs

Purpose:

To discover the basic needs of humans and how they are satisfied.

To discover why some humans cannot satisfy their basic needs.

To encourage concern for humans who cannot satisfy their basic needs.

To develop map skills, vocabulary, thinking and independent learning skills.

**Remember to put a task number by each answer in your Journal.
Tick each box when the task is finished.**

Reinforcement of the teacher's expectations

Tasks:

❏ 1 Study pages 1 to 3 in the gold coloured "Food and Survival Book 1". Answer question 1 on page 3.

Get help from Task Card 3.1 if you need it.

Students don't need to wait for help from the teacher

❏ 2 Answer either question 2 or question 3.

❏ 3 Read "How to survive a shipwreck" on page 4 of the booklet. Answer the question on that page.

Ticks in boxes show the pace at which students are working

Task Card 3.3 will help.

❏ 4 Organise yourself into groups of 5. Work as a group to complete Groupsheet 3, "What is Economics about?".

This is an example of a contract which helps to ensure that students stay on task; it would be appropriate with sixth-form students, for example.

FLEXIBLE LEARNING CONTRACT

Name: _____ Subject: _____

Tutor: _____ Topic: _____

Learning Objectives	Standards Expected

Clarification of what is to be done

Tutorial Times	Study Time	
	School	Home

Timescales (to be negotiated)

Total time for activity

Resources to be used

Signed _____ (Student) Date: _____

Signed: _____ (Tutor) Date: _____

Identifying the outputs a task leads to

Students have different aptitudes, which can be demonstrated in the way they present the product of an activity. To allow differentiation, tasks need to be designed so they enable a variety of outputs.

Lessons in English

A   The class reads extracts from *Thunder and Lightnings*, by Jan Mark.

B   The class is divided into groups, each of which examines one character and discusses the issues he or she faces, the type of character he or she is, the involvement in the plot and the style of writing.

C   The groups are then asked to select an episode from the book involving their character, and to rehearse the episode and produce a still photograph or freeze frame. They perform their episodes and the rest of the class question the participants about their roles, feelings and intentions.

D   The class are then asked to focus on Mitch Milligan, the hero of the book, in best comic book traditions. Pupils work in groups on different tasks:

   –   Some analyse comics which portray heroes, negotiate agreed criteria and produce a database reflecting their research into the common characteristics of heroes and heroines

   –   Some recast the story as a storyboard for TV or a comic strip

   –   Some analyse the character and represent him through a TV interview, or contributions to a radio programme

   –   Some promote a cause or issue raised in the text, involving the character, through a poster, pamphlet or radio documentary

   –   Some create a book poster or book-jacket.

Variety of outputs to allow individual strengths to emerge

E   The different tasks lead groups to produce text, audio, video and display material. The class is brought back together to examine the conventions used in text, audio and visual material to represent heroes and heroines. They finish the section of work by producing their own short chapter from a book involving a hero, either in the archetypal mode or presented quite differently.

West Sussex LEA

Allowing choice in tasks

Allowing students choice in the tasks they carry out will enable them to develop their differing aptitudes and interests. Discretion will obviously need to be used by the teacher, however, so that students do not make unsuitable choices.

LESSONS IN SCIENCE

A   Initially, the class is given a few questions about investigating forces and energy by using toy vehicles. They are asked to extend the list and build up a set of questions like:

- are bigger cars faster?

- do plastic cars go faster than metal cars?

- does a long-life battery make a car go faster than an ordinary battery?

- is a clockwork motor better than a battery powered motor?

- are large wheels better than small wheels?

- is carpet a better surface than vinyl for testing cars?

- does the length of the test route matter?

- does the number of turns to a clockwork car affect its maximum speed?

- what difference do tyres make?

- what is the heaviest load a car can pull?

- does the colour of a car matter?

- which car needs the largest force to start it?

B   The class is invited to list the questions in the order of perceived difficulty.

C   Groups are then organised to undertake (with guided choice) certain of the investigations. All must note how they approach the problem, and organise their investigations and their findings scientifically. They report back in a mixture of text, tables and display diagrams.

D   A final class session draws out principles and conclusions.

Students define their own area of investigation

Students are allowed choice in the complexity of the investigation

Students choose investigations to ensure ownership of the task

This provides teachers with the opportunity to 'stretch' indivdual students

National Curriculum Council

Learning Routes

Some teachers design modules which cater for different levels of ability, by designing ability-specific tasks. The route a student takes depends on individual ability. One drawback with this approach is that it may reinforce teacher expectation of performance.

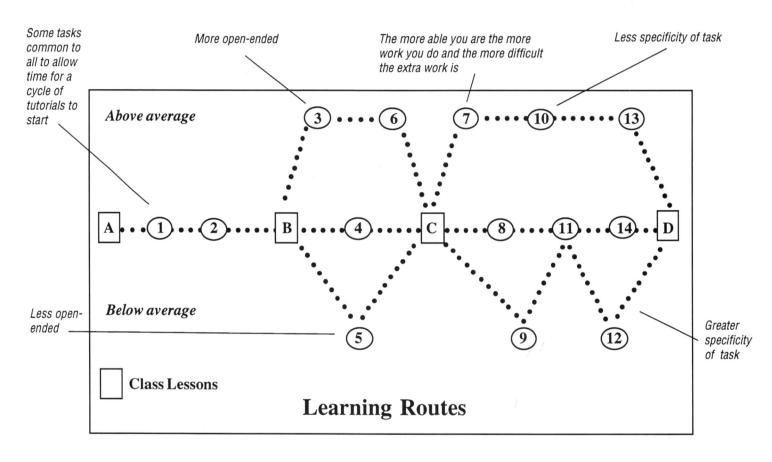

Learning Routes

Differentiation by Support

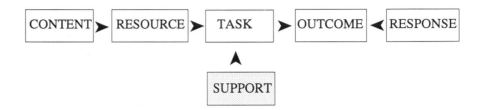

```
CONTENT ➤ RESOURCE ➤ TASK ➤ OUTCOME ◀ RESPONSE
                       ▲
                    SUPPORT
```

We know that some students need more help than others to complete a given task. If we provide help we are also providing differentiation by support. The six strategies suggested in this section provide guidance on how differentiation by support may be given more systematically. These strategies are:

1 Support from other adults and students
2 Individual support from the teacher
3 Support from carefully selected systems and technology
4 Celebration of achievement
5 Cooperative teaching
6 Small group tutoring

The first five of these strategies are illustrated by the example below, which comes from a school in Coventry.

Poetry Assignment

The aims of the work were:

– to produce a class file of poetry from established poets and from the class which would cover a range of writing
– to consider some abstract ideas about the nature of poetry as a starting point to the file
– to assess students' skills in poetry writing, involvement with and enjoyment of poetry.

A year 8 mixed-ability class with two teachers carried out this work – the class's own English teacher and a support teacher working with a Records of Achievement brief – over 5 weeks. Planning time was given by the school before the project began. The pattern of work was as follows:

1 The class were given at random a statement about the nature of poetry. These ranged in difficulty: some concepts were simple – "poems are fun", others complex – "Poetry is the synthesis of hyacinths and biscuits". Students were asked to seek support, and talk through their statement till they came to an understanding of it. If it proved too difficult, they would be 'dealt' a new statement and start again. Much purposeful talk followed till understandings were reached.

2 They then had to find a poem which best illustrated their statement. The room was filled with poetry books alongside the usual class library materials. Students researched the materials available, and made visits to the library. Teachers were asked for guidance/advice on best choices.

3 Once the class had decided on some aspects of poetry, they were asked to write some of their own. Then followed a sequence of lessons in which patterns and ideas for poems were given based on Sandy Brownjohn's book.* Some students wrote one poem, others five or six – all were collected in the class file. A word processor was on hand for group drafting of ideas, students negotiating its use for themselves. A tape recorder was available for oral 'drafting' of ideas.

4 Students then returned to other published poems, chose those which they enjoyed and discussed which poems to include.

5 Other published poems were used as a stimulus for further student writings.

6 The file grew and was celebrated. It was read by students who commented on each other's work, was shown to every visitor to the classroom, and was available for display on parents' evening. Unsolicited poems, written at home, were brought in by students. A nearby primary school working on poetry heard of the file, so they sent their poems for students to comment on.

7 The class made a 'boaster poster' in which they 'shouted' their achievements. All the students wrote a sentence on what they felt they had achieved.

8 Some members of the class wrote letters to both teachers, spontaneously expressing their enjoyment of the project and demanding that it be repeated. Teachers replied.

9 The file joined the class library materials for general reading.

Small Group Tutoring

At its simplest, differentiation by support may come down to the talks you have with your students. Whilst support for individual students is a vital ingredient in differentiated teaching, you will need to be aware of a number of constraints:

- lack of time will prevent you from supporting all students in this way
- some students are intimidated by one-to-one conversation with the teacher
- individual conversation of this type will not facilitate the flow of ideas between group members.

* *Does it have to Rhyme?* by Sandy Brownjohn, Hodder & Stoughton, 1980

To overcome these difficulties, some teachers are adopting the strategy of small group tutoring. This can support students by ensuring that they have clarity about the nature of the task and how they might tackle it. The following example is a transcript from a video sequence (*Supporting Students in Flexible Learning*, NCET/SCET, 1991) and shows how a year 7 maths class begin an individual investigation based on a box of Smarties.

Tutor	Following our investigation we need to decide as a group what everyone is going to do, and know exactly what everyone is doing. So what ideas have you got?
Steven	I want to know how many Smarties there are in the box, we are going to do bar charts.
Tutor	So you are checking all the information from all the class. So what are you going to do then?
Naweeda	I am getting all the information from the class.
Tutor	You remember last time when we did the other one it was really difficult, wasn't it? So you need to be prepared, what are you doing first of all?
Naweeda	I am going to write down the names and when I've asked them I am going to cross out their names, so we know we have asked them.
Tutor	So what information are you going to record?
Naweeda	How many Smarties, what are the most Smarties. Ask what the most popular colour is.
Tutor	Biggest number there is. You are going to look at just how many Smarties they have got in a box or anything else?
Naweeda	Just how many Smarties there are in a box.
Tutor	So you are not going to ask them about colours?
Naweeda	No.
Carley	Going to ask what the most popular colour is and just mark it off to tell us what we've got and come back here and do a bar graph.
Tutor	So you are going to mark them off the bar graph. What are you going to do then if they have got three blue ones and three yellow ones?
Carley	I'm going to ask which one they prefer.
Tutor	You are not asking them how many there are, the biggest number, you are asking...
Carley	Which ones they think are the most popular.
Tutor	Sorry, I misunderstood what you are doing. So you are asking them which colour they like best, everyone. What are you doing then, Darren?
Darren	I'm going to weigh all the Smarties.
Teacher	What, everybody's?
Darren	Going to divide it by the number of boxes to get an average.
Tutor	If Darren is doing that, and working out the weight of one Smarties, do you think that is going to be accurate doing it that way?
Paul	No.
Tutor	Well how could it be more accurate? I thought it was really good.
Paul	He can weigh one.
Tutor	Where? You think weighing one is more accurate than the way he is doing it?
Darren	Yes.
Tutor	Right, let's talk about this as a group then. We want to know the weight of one Smartie, and we want it to be as accurate as possible. Let us think about how we can make it as accurate as possible. Paul is saying that we weigh one Smartie, and Darren is saying that he weighs a whole box and divides it by how many Smarties there are. Why do you want to do it that way, why do you think that is more accurate?
Paul	It's not more accurate because they all weigh the same.
Tutor	So what is wrong with just weighing one, what is the problem with just weighing one?
Paul	Too light for our scales.
Tutor	So getting an average is better. Do you think that is better, are you sure now?
Carley	We won't weigh the box, just the Smarties.
Tutor	If Darren is weighing one box of Smarties and finding the average, could we be even more accurate than that?
Steven	We could weigh more boxes, we could go round all the tables.
Tutor	So we could weigh all your tables together, shall we see if we get different answers? So put your heading 'weight', so you know what you are doing for weight.
Paul	Miss, I'm going to do a pie chart.
Tutor	Right, we have got a weighing experiment going . . . what else are you going to do?

Differentiation by Response

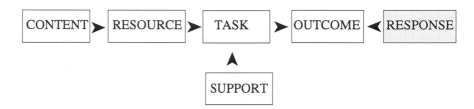

Even when they work on a common task, the products of any group of students will exhibit differences. This is what we mean by differentiated outcomes. Each individual has a unique combination of strengths and weaknesses and so the work of each will need to be responded to differently.

In this section we suggest seven strategies that you might look at to develop differentiation by response. These are:

1 Making course objectives accessible
2 Making assessment criteria explicit
3 Creating a system of response partners
4 Providing learning logs
5 Small group tutoring
6 Individual action plans
7 Ensuring that response reflects what the student has achieved.

Making course objectives accessible

An advanced organiser is the equivalent of the picture on the box lid of a jigsaw puzzle. It gives the students a picture of what it is they are trying to achieve. Such a picture is necessary if students are to understand how the teacher's response to their work relates to the task they were given.

The example below is the advanced organiser for the activity referred to previously on page 7.

LESSONS IN HUMANITIES

The aims are to:

– extend and apply pupils' knowledge of the school community and link it to a school in India

– offer opportunities to extend pupils' knowledge of the school's relationship to other places in the home region

– learn how particular human activity has altered the landscape

– develop pupils' appreciation of how others contribute to the school community

– improve pupils' knowledge of the wider world

Often we keep course objectives to ourselves. By making them accessible to students we are able to relate our response to what was required in a way that is meaningful to the student.

Making assessment criteria explicit

The following examples come from teachers in Dudley. They show how they made explicit the assessment criteria for different ability groups working on the same activity.

The purpose of the following task may be common, but the criteria for assessment will be particular to the needs, interests and abilities of individuals.

Teachers should plan to include times which give opportunities for differentiated responses to be made to students.

Red Group: Use these targets to help improve your work!		
Sentences	5b	I can write using accurate use of sentences and structural punctuation
	6b	I can write and include accurate use of commas, brackets, dashes
Drafting	5d	I can gather ideas on paper/V.D.U. and produce a draft from these, revising if necessary
	6d	I can draft independently, taking appropriate action
Presentation	6c	I can use different ways to present my work, eg Art, graphics, D.T.P.
Stories	4b	I can write stories with openings, characters, settings, events, end, and gaining interest
Purpose	5e	I can discuss the differences in vocabulary, depending on the purpose and audience.
Checklist	5b	
	6b	
	5d	
	6d	
	6c	
	4b	
	5e	
Group Meeting _____ date _____ time _____		

Yellow Group: Let's talk about these ideas
Can you put them in your writing?

1. Is the writing clear and joined up?
2. Is my writing done in sentences?
3. Have I used Capital letters and full stops?
4. Have I asked for help with spellings?
5. Can I tell Mrs Bates my ideas for my story?
6. Does my story have a beginning, middle and end?
7. Does my story have characters in it?
8. Does it have events... how many?
9. Who have I written my story for?
10. I can read my story to Mrs Bates and my friend.

Teachers should plan to include times which give opportunities for differentiated responses to be made to students.

Response partners

This work, developed by Somerset teachers, allows students to respond to one another's work. With objectives and assessment criteria made available to them, students can discuss their work. Often putting thoughts into words helps the student who is having to make a response as well as the student who is receiving it.

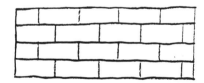

Ever talked to a brick wall?
It doesn't do much good you know! Unless the wall is helpful and full of advice.

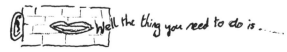
Well the thing you need to do is _____.

Too often, though, walls don't answer back,
This is where human beings come in handy! They can be ...

...Response Partners.1

What is a Response Partner ?

This is the posh title for the person who helps you with your writing. You read each others work and offer advice on it.

Why ?

The idea is then that you try to improve.

How ?

By using your Response Partner you can get an idea of how a reader feels about your work. He or she can point out things you may have missed or just not thought of. You then read the work of your partner and try to help them in the same way.

It is often a good idea to bounce ideas off each other to test them and see if they have value.

What to say about another's writing. (Some Ideas.)

I liked the ending.
I like these words ____
How did you get this idea ?
Why did you write that ?
I thought this was very strong --- powerful !
This is realistic.
You've got that across well.
You haven't got that across very well.
Good beginning
You need a stronger beginning.
You build up the atmosphere well.
You got me involved in the story.
This is a well written character.
This character needs more work.
Why did you write that bit like that ?
Are you happy with the bit where ___ ?
These are golden lines.
Fantastic !

Oh do you really think so ?

Providing learning logs

Teachers will want to respond to the ways in which students are working as much as to the quality of what they are doing. If this is to be effective, it requires that students also pay attention to the ways in which they are working – students will need to think about their thinking, and learn about their learning. One way of doing this is through the use of learning logs. These may simply be spaces in a homework diary or a small 'vocabulary' book. Towards the end of each lesson, time is made available for students to reflect upon the lesson. These reflections are recorded in the learning log and become an additional source in guiding the teacher's response.

Small group tutoring

As with the previous section on differentiation by support, responding to students' work may often be fulfilled by finding time for detailed conversations with them. In finding time you have to juggle two variables: length of discussion and frequency. If discussion relates to individual performance against assessment criteria, it is likely to be lengthy; moving on to discussing strategies for improvement and involving action planning requires even more time. This is likely to result in contact time being very infrequent.

Small group tutoring is one strategy available, providing more support than class teaching, whilst addressing time constraints.

For a full account of this approach, you may find it useful to see the video package *Supporting Students in Flexible Learning,* published by NCET/ SCET, 1991.

Individual Action Plans

To be effective, differentiation by response requires that students incorporate the teacher's ideas in future action. Individual action plans are one way of formalising this, as the example overleaf shows.

for PRACTICAL PROJECT

Name .... Tutor Group ....

Course .... Art 'A' level .... Target Exam Grade .... A/B ....

Areas of study .. Drawing method/composition/markmaking/tone

Project title .. Monochromatic study .. Target project grade .. B ....

Strengths identified, with suggestions for further development

AREA identified as a STRENGTH .. Drawing method (very accurate)

IDEAS for DEVELOPMENT .. Not too confident about applying this method with a different subject e.g. figures

STRATEGIES (ie EXERCISES) .. 2x single figure drawings, using my current method - A3, pencil. HOMEWORK

DEADLINE DATE .. 11/11/92

AREA(S) identified as PROBLEMS ① Tone - not enough variation
② Markmaking - ok for some surfaces, but not all

Problems identified with strategies for improvement

IDEAS for IMPROVEMENT .. ① Tone - more exploration exercises
② Practise different surfaces, eg foliage

STRATEGIES (ie EXERCISES) ① Fill A5 sheet with sample weights of pencil marks - B, HB, 2B, 4B HOMEWORK
② 3x direct observation studies of foliage

Deadlines

DEADLINE DATES .. ① Tone - 11/11/92 ② Markmaking 18/11/92

PAIR GRADE AWARDED .. C+

DATE .. 24/10/92

DATE OF GROUP REVIEW SESSION .. 4/11/92

Hyde Sixth-Form College

30

Ensuring that response reflects what the student has achieved

Improvement in the quality of student's work is individual, and may only be gradual. To be effective, teacher response should respond to an individual's work based on past achievement, rather than on measurement against an abstract idea.

HSFC ART DEPT. STUDENT INDUCTION SHEET 2		
Art A Level skills		Where am I?
The skills I Need:	Where am I now: Practiced?	Confident
a Think CREATIVELY Think LOGICALLY	Art, 3D work in GCSE / Design in graphics Planning design etc in graphics	Confident in creative thinking in certain areas. Confident as I was able to overcome most design problems
b PROBLEM-SOLVING	Product design, etc in graphics (shopping centre design)	Confident as I've had to solve practical problems
c An understanding of the VISUAL LANGUAGE 1 Drawing methods 2 Colour 3 Markmaking 4 Composition	Experience in using different equipment practised in different areas. Tried various techniques such as abstract, pointillism etc work experience at Design Studio	Confident as I've tried different equipment in both Art and Graphics such as pastels, paint, crayon, airbrush. Got an A in both Art and Graphics
d Express a PERSONAL POINT OF VIEW	English essays on various subjects such as abortion, animal rights	Very confident Grade A in Eng. lang
e Record from DIRECT OBSERVATION	Done still life painting/drawings in Art	Good grades for pieces
f RESEARCH from DIRECT SOURCES	Spoken to designers on work experience Spoke to artist and Art students	Confident
RESEARCH from OTHER SOURCES	Read books and magazines. Watched programmes on Art and Design	Very confident as I read a lot.

Hyde Sixth-Form College

31

Appendix A

INSET Activity

This activity has proved helpful when teachers first begin to raise, and share, awareness of differentiation. It is intended to provoke discussion and could be used at departmental or whole school meetings.

ACTIVITY

1   Overleaf are ten statements about differentiation.

Examine each statement in turn.

Decide whether the statement is referring to

input

process

outcome

and group the statements accordingly.

2   Work with a colleague on this activity.

Using the same ten statements, produce a rank order of importance on the following lines:

1st

2nd   2nd

3rd   3rd   3rd

4th   4th

5th

One card will have to be discarded.

Justify your rank order.

For obvious reasons this is called a Diamond Nine exercise.

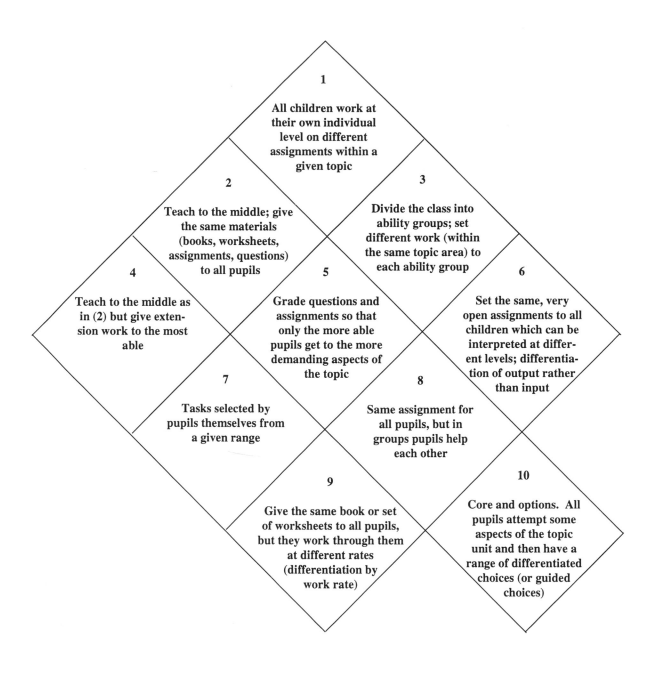

The diamond nine activity

Appendix B

Checklists

Resource

We have identified seven strategies that could be used to aid differentiation by resource. Which are you already making use of? If you are already making use of some of these strategies tick the appropriate boxes.

1 Resources related for: appropriate readability levels ☐
                                          ease of use by students ☐
                                          good design ☐

2 Wide variety of media ☐

3 Use of technology ☐

4 Use of study guides ☐

5 Well managed storage and retrieval systems ☐

6 Student preparation ☐

7 Study skills built into course programmes ☐

Task

We have identified six strategies that could be used to aid differentiation by task.

Which are you already making use of?

1 Providing a variety of tasks. ☐

2 Matching of tasks to student abilities, aptitudes and interests. ☐

3 Ensuring students stay on task. ☐

4 Identifying the outputs tasks lead to. ☐

5 Providing a range of tasks to allow choice. ☐

6 Building learning routes. ☐

Support   We have identified six strategies that could be used to aid differentiation by support.

Which are you already making use of?

1 Support from other adults and students.   ☐
2 Individual support from the teacher.   ☐
3 Support from carefully resourced systems and technology.   ☐
4 Celebration of achievement.   ☐
5 Cooperative teaching.   ☐
6 Small group tutoring.   ☐

Response   We have identified seven strategies that could be used to aid differentiation by response.

Which are you already making use of?

1 Making course objectives accessible to students   ☐
2 Making assessment criteria explicit   ☐
3 Response partners   ☐
4 Learning logs   ☐
5 Small group tutoring   ☐
6 Individual action plans   ☐
7 Response reflects what the student has previously achieved ☐

Appendix C

Action Planning

One of the strategies we can use with students to provide differentiation is to Action Plan future developments, paying close attention to their present circumstances and achievements.

Now it's your turn to do this, and below we provide a series of questions to guide your future individual Action Planning.

1 Check Where You Are Now

Copy this chart for each group or subject you teach. Place a tick in the appropriate box/es.

Group ....

Subject. ....

In my classroom practice I differentiate by:

	Frequently	Often	Sometimes	Never
Resource	☐	☐	☐	☐
Task	☐	☐	☐	☐
Support	☐	☐	☐	☐
Response	☐	☐	☐	☐

2 Choose to Change where it's Easiest for You

You may find some types of differentiation easier to manage in one subject or with one group than another. This may depend on how you feel about class size, and the frequency or length of teaching periods. Use the space below to note in which class/es you would wish to increase differentiation within your teaching.

	Group	Subject (if appropriate)	Unit of Work
1	....	....	....
2	....	....	....
3	....	....	....
4	....	....	....

Now think about which methods of differentiation would be suitable in your circumstances. Tick any that are appropriate:

Resource ☐   Support ☐

Task ☐   Response ☐

3 You Must be Realistic

When you are beginning to change your classroom practice it's best to only attempt one thing at a time. We would recommend that you select *one* teaching group and *one* method of differentiation to begin with. Which of the strategies we have suggested will you use? You need to consider what help you may need and which resources might assist you.

_____

_____

_____

What timescale would make sense for this activity?

Action	Length of time required	Complete by when?

4 Check Back

Identify the sections of this handbook which will help you with planning the work you have described above.

_____

_____

_____

5 How Did It Go? (Use this section after a predetermined interval)

Review your progress from time to time and reflect on the changes you have made to your classroom practice.

_____

_____

_____

Appendix D

A Selected List of References

Classroom Management, Waterhouse P., Network Educational Press, 1990

Differentiation, Your Responsibility: an Inservice Training Pack for Staff Development, National Association of Remedial Education (NARE), 1991

Flexible Learning: an Outline, Waterhouse P., Network Educational Press, 1990

Implementing Flexible Learning: a Resource Pack for Trainers, NEC/NCET, 1989

Information Skills in the Secondary School Curriculum, Marland M., Methuen Educational, 1981

Mixed Ability Work in Comprehensive Schools, Department of Education and Science, 1979, HMSO

Modern Foreign Languages in the National Curriculum: Non-Statutory Guidance for Teachers, Curriculum Council for Wales, 1992

Resources for Flexible Learning, Powell R., Network Educational Press, 1990

Science and Pupils with Special Educational Needs: A Workshop Pack for Key Stage 1 & 2, NCC INSET Resources, 1991

Supported Self-Study: an Introduction for Teachers, Waterhouse P., NCET, 1988

Supported Self-Study at National Curriculum Key Stage 3, NCET, 1990

Supporting Students in Flexible Learning: a Practical Look at Classroom Management and Tutoring Skills, (video training pack), NCET/SCET, 1991

Tutoring, Waterhouse P., Network Educational Press, 1990